Your Guide to

bringing more

acts of Self care

Workbook

> *" Self Care and Self Love are so important
> in the Evolution of You "*
> *-Becoming Unique*

My Name is Unique, yup that's my real name given to me by my mother and father at birth.

I am the author of this book. I never in my wildest dreams would have thought that I would be an author.

I was a kid that was left back in second grade and pulled out of class to go to resource room and speech therapy. School was not an easy task for me. I had to work 10 times harder than my counter parts to just be a C student. Speech was a challenge for me. I heard many times through my childhood the giggles because my pronunciation on some words would sound different. Other kids would say, why you talk like that. I even remember in high school, a friend at that time couldn't understand something I said and responded to me, "I hope you don't teach your kids how to talk"

I don't recall ever saying out loud I'm not good enough to be an author. But looking back now I subconsciously grew to believe I wasn't good enough to do such. How could I now entertain that idea?

The answer is SELF LOVE!!!! Through self care actions, my self love grew to learn to accept and love all parts of myself just as I am.

I wrote this book by myself. I did not want a ghost writer to bring my ideas out. I wanted my voice to bring my ideas out. As you read this book, you may bump into some overrun sentences here and there or maybe a comma is missing. I wrote this book in the spirit of pure passion and LOVE to share a message. I did not want to block my message because of grammar. Plus I wanted to be true to my real life voice. You won't find any big or complicated words here. What you will find are simple words with life changing tools.

I am living proof that we have the power to change the narrative that we have created for ourselves through self care......

TABLE OF CONTENTS

You are an important person in your own life!!!!! 1

Week 1: Chapter 1 - Prepare 3

Week 2: Chapter 2 - Affirmations 11

Week 3: Chapter 3 - Journaling. 21

Week 4: Chapter 4 - Small acts of self care 29

Week 5: Chapter 5 - Breathing 39

Week 6: Chapter 6 - Guided meditation 43

Week 7: Chapter 7 - Meditation. 49

Week 8: Chapter 8 - Movement 55

Week 9: Chapter 9 - Review 61

Week 10: Chapter 10 - Pamper Time 79

Week 11: Chapter 11 - Excitement 83

Week 12: Chapter 12 - Your Happy Place 89

Journaling Pages for You. 93

You are an important person in your own life!!!!!

I want to start this book off with the reminder that you are indeed IMPORTANT!!!!!

Your guide to bringing more acts of self care workbook is a Start, a Refresher or a Push to pick up on your self care. This book will offer tools for you to create space, and understanding around your individual self care practices. Workbook is technically what this book is called because you are expected to put the work in with yourself. No matter where you are in your self care routine or lifestyle there will be tools here for the beginner to be introduced to, and for the experienced to work with.

If you are reading this, it means you are in search to add more Self Care, which in turn grows into Self Love. To search for more self care doesnt mean self love is missing, but by allowing time and space for YOU- with gifting Self Care to yourself,

Self Love will be magnified. Introducing more acts of Self Care into one's life is such a beautiful place to be.

Self care is a time and opportunity for us to learn ourselves so we can thrive in our own lives. It's about honoring who you are.

This book will be a tool to help you tap into your own energies, and be in alignment with how you want to show up in your world.

Lifestyle changes and Self Care changes don't happen overnight, it happens over time! This book will not be a read in one day book or one week, but this will be a workbook that you will work through over the next 90 days (3 months)

Each section of the book will allow you to work through the process of adding more Self Care into your life. This workbook will not be telling you to get a manicure or facial as acts of self care. Instead this book will offer acts of self care as part of your everyday lifestyle. Or as one of my "Becoming Unique" Podcast guest called it the "Wellness Diet"

Before you dive into this book, I ask that you hold grace for yourself. Don't look for perfection, but instead be grateful for progress.

CHAPTER 1

Prepare!!!!!

This is like your Welcome Week at school. We are not going to dive into the lesson plan just yet, but we are going to get organized, and prepare ourselves for what's ahead.

-- ***Buy a journal*** (Put intention into the purchase of the journal that you buy or use)

Take this week to prepare by buying a journal or notebook. Decline the urge to pick up any journal or notebook just to get started. Treat this purchase with respect. Give this transaction the same energy as you would give the selection of a gift that you were giving someone to impress. When you pick up the journal or notebook before purchase, ask yourself "what do I

3

like about this journal?" This journal will be your right hand man with this book so be conscious of all details from the way the pages turn to the visual look of the cover.

Moving and acting with loving intention is an act of self care/ self love. This journal/notebook is a gift to yourself, enjoy the process of selecting, buying and preparing to use it.

You will also need pens and highlighters as well. Use the same energy in selecting a pen as you do with the selection of your journal. Do you like the way the pen gildes on the paper when you write? Does the pen ink stop flowing when you write sideways and you may have to shake the pen up for it to start working again? These are questions to ask yourself to aid in you having smooth transactions with your journal and pen. You wouldn't want to be in the flow of ideas, thoughts with writing in your journal then all of a sudden your pen starts to have complications with writing and you have to interrupt to shake up your pen or look for a new one. Be ready with a good writing pen.

In the end, be ready to highlight noteworthy information with your highlighter in this book, and have your pen always ready to answer questions in your journal.

*-- **Take Inventory of your home.*** Where can you have a private space of your own to meditate, be still, be quiet? Or maybe you live in a smaller space like an NYC apartment where having a private space could be challenging with a family or roommates around. Then question yourself on what times of the day works best for your quiet moments? Start to mentally map all of this out.

*-- **Understanding the definition of the following words.*** There are words in our language that we may know and use, but have we really sat in that word to understand it on a deeper level. Here are a couple of words that we will be using throughout the book and it is key that you don't just read or hear the words, but you embody these words.

Words to Embody

Mindfulness -- to be conscious or aware of something, in the moment, your environment, emotions, someone else.........

We have the opportunity to be mindful in all parts of our lives, but how many times do we skip, or overlook a moment because our mind is somewhere else. Are we giving ourselves the present of being PRESENT? Are you living in the moment or thinking about what someone said to you 2 weeks ago, or

maybe thinking about things in the future that haven't even happened yet?

Here are a couple of examples of how you can bring mindfulness in your everyday actions.

Food -- Our bodies are nourished by the foods that we put in it. If you don't already practice mindful eating, be mindful to practice mindfulness eating with at least one meal a day or a week, find your personal rhythm. Remove distractions such as the TV, your phone....(if you are watching TV or playing with your phone, there is less attention to your food, and attention on the outside distractions) Your food deserves your attention, it's about to nourish your cells and body, be open to be present with your food, and pour mindful energy into it. Ways to be present with your food are to be aware of the smell, and the taste. As you chew your food, be present with the flavors, do you taste pepper, lemon, what seasonings are flowing through your tastebuds? How's the texture? Does your food bring memories of your childhood, or other personal memories? Be mindful of judgements and just experience what is. Take note of what you like about this moment, be in the moment, experience what your food has to offer you.

Emotions -- Another example of a way to practice mindfulness could be in your *emotions*. If you are having a moment of being snippy at people or have an attitude towards others, this is an opportunity to be mindful. Why are you feeling the feelings you are feeling? There is not one answer, or is it always the other person's fault. Check in with yourself. Be mindful of your emotions, you may be upset about waking up late and having a rough start to your day, and in turn it manifests into having an attitude. Instead become mindful of your emotions, acknowledge them, and allow yourself grace.

We have the opportunity to practice mindfulness throughout all of our actions daily. Start to embody more mindfulness practices in your preparation week as this word will come up in this book more than one time.

Holding Grace for yourself -- There is no such thing as perfection so please throw perfection thoughts out the window, and be open to hold grace for yourself in this book. To hold grace for yourself is to give yourself permission to be okay with where you are at in the present moment. It's okay to make mistakes, and not do things perfectly. Be open to grow and learn during a process. Be kind to yourself always. Treat yourself as you would expect others to treat you. Embody the idea of holding grace for yourself!

Affirmations -- The action of Affirming something.

"I Am" when put together are two of the most powerful words in the English language because whatever words follow it has the opportunity to become your reality. Be mindful of how you use "I am" because inturn you are affirming your spoken words. Be mindful of the self talk that you have been having with yourself. Have you been affirming negative self talk with 'I am'? For example- Do you say things like "I AM not smart enough for that job" or"I AM not small enough to wear that outfit" These don't have to be your exact dialog, but these are examples on how easy it is to affirm negative affirmations upon yourself. Affirmations is the second chapter but before we reach there I invite you to sit in and embody the power of Affirmations. I invite you to go to the internet, and search and listen to some positive affirmation videos as you get ready for your day. Remember Embody what an affirmation is!

Review

-Embody the words spoken above. *(Mindfulness, Holding Grace for Yourself & Affirmations)*

-Listen to affirmations on the internet or your streaming music apps.

-Mark a date on your calendar when you are ready to start your journey into this book. Once you marked the date and the date arrives, open up to Chapter 2.

Be sure to have your journal, pen and highlighter with *Your Guide to Bringing more acts of Self Care Workbook* at all times. You will have the opportunity to respond to questions directly in the workbook, but it is suggested that you use your personal journal for your responses to the questions and prompts in this book. Using your personal journal for responses will allow you to dig deeper into your responses to the questions or prompts in this book. You will be able to respond to prompts without the restriction of the few small lines provided in this book. This self care experience will be a place of digging deeper than the surface. Your responses will require more than yes or no answers, and it is key to being open to writing your responses in your personal journal.

CHAPTER 2

Affirmations!!!!

Before we jump right into Affirmations, I have a couple of questions. Did you do all your preparation in chapter one? Did you embody the vocabulary?

Welcome to week two. This week is all about Affirmations. Each week we will be adding new lifestyle self care, self loving practices to our routines. Once we move on to the next week by introducing a new practice, we will not forget about the previous week's practice. Each week you will continue to practice the previous week's practices on your own. There will not always be reminders of the previous chapters once you arrive at the new weekly chapter so it will be up to you to

continue the work of each week as we move along with each newer chapter.

Let's get started

In this chapter, each day will be a set of new affirmations. Feel free to highlight, or circle the ones that resonate with you the most. By the end of the week, you will create your own set of affirmations from the affirmations that resonated with you. Say these affirmations outloud to yourself at least 3 times each.

DAY 1 (AFFIRMATIONS)

I am worthy of a beautiful life

I am a blessing

I love myself

I am enough

I am _____

(fill in the blank)

Question:

How do you feel about saying affirmations to yourself?

_____

_____

_____

_____

_____

_____

_____

_____

_____

_____

_____

DAY 2 (AFFIRMATIONS)

If any of Day one affirmations resonated with you, go ahead and highlight, circle or write them into your journal.

Let's move into Day two affirmations

> *I am Loved*
>
> *I am Magic*
>
> *I am perfect just as I am*
>
> *I am enough*
>
> *I am _____*
>
> *(Fill in the blank)*

Question:

Do you believe the affirmations when you say them to yourself? (This is your personal journal, be honest with yourself) Whatever your answer is, take a moment to ponder and write. It's always great to question ourselves and dig deeper.

_____

_____

_____

_____

_____

DAY 3 (AFFIRMATIONS)

Remember to collect the affirmations that resonate with you by highlighting, circling or putting them in your journal book. Remember to say these affirmations out loud at least three times.

> *I am a Rockstar*
>
> *I am one of a kind*
>
> *I am braver than I think*
>
> *I am enough*
>
> *I am* _____
>
> *(Fill in the blank)*

Question:

Just write whatever thoughts are in your mind after reading today"s affirmations

_____

_____

_____

_____

_____

_____

Day 4 (Affirmations)

I think you are getting a hang of the routine. Say your affirmations out loud. Take note of the affirmations that are resonating with you. Let's go.....

> *I am capable of amazing things*
>
> *I have great ideas*
>
> *I am flawless just the way I am*
>
> *I am enough*
>
> *I am* _____
>
> *(Fill in the blank)*

Question:

Are you getting used to saying affirmations?

_____

_____

_____

_____

_____

_____

_____

_____

DAY 5 (AFFIRMATIONS)

I think you are becoming a pro at I am affirmations, let's drop the "I am" now. Same routine, say the affirmattions at least three times each, and take notes on what's resonating with you.

> *I deserve to be happy*
>
> *I believe in myself*
>
> *I accept all of me*
>
> *I honor my life*
>
> *I* _____
>
> *(fill in the blank)*

Question:

Talk about the affirmation that you used to fill in the blank

_____

_____

_____

_____

_____

_____

_____

_____

Day 6 (Affirmations)

You know the drill

> *Today I choose Joy*
>
> *Today I am not affected by the judgment of others*
>
> *Today I deserved to be Loved by myself*
>
> *Today I honor myself with knowing that I am Enough*
>
> *Today _____*
>
> *(fill in the blank)*

Question:

Do you like starting your affirmations with " Today I" ? (Why or why not)

_____

_____

_____

_____

_____

_____

_____

_____

_____

DAY 7 (AFFIRMATIONS)

Be proud of yourself! You have said affirmations to yourself for the past 6 days. Take a moment to applaud yourself and sit in the moment of the self caring and loving work that you have gifted yourself with.

Now let's talk about Day 7 Affirmations. You are now the creator.

Write your own five daily affirmations today. You can choose some from the past six days of affirmations or you can choose your own or both. Whatever you decide, have confidence in your time to customize your unique set of affirmations for you to carry on into your daily life routine of self care and self love. Feel free to go back to any of the affirmations at any time and feel free to change your affirmations daily if need be.

1. _____

2. _____

3. _____

4. _____

5. _____

No question today. Once again applaud yourself for showing up for you and the commitment that you have given yourself over the past seven days. You are a Rockstar

CHAPTER 3

Journaling!!!!!!!

Welcome to week three of adding more acts of self care into your lifestyle. This week is all about journaling, but don't forget about your affirmations from week two. I will not talk about affirmations in this chapter, but it's up to you to add them into your lifestyle when needed. Maybe it will become part of your morning routine or you use them when you are feeling low and you need to boost yourself up with some positive high vibrational words. This is your life so it's up to you to see how to customize these new practices in a way that they resonate with you.

What is journaling? Journaling is simply writing down your thoughts, feelings and ideas to work through them to be able to understand them more clearly. If you struggle with anxiety or depression or stress, journaling could be a great tool. When you feel you have no one to talk to or you want to dump your thoughts and emotions, journaling is a great resource.

Everyone's journaling journey can look different as we are all uniquely created individuals. The reason why I may show up to write in my journal could be completely different from the reason you show up to your journal. There is no wrong or right way to journal, it's very individualistic. There is just something very magical and therapeutic about bringing your thoughts, emotions, stresses, worries, ideas and so much more to pen and paper.

If you are new to journaling, be open to try this even if you have had some reservations about it. (Try it, you may like it.) If you are already a pro at this journaling practice, please do follow along with class. You never know, you may pick up something new.

This chapter is 7 days long. Seven days of showing up with your pen and paper. Journaling does not have to be an everyday practice or it could be an everyday practice. In the end, it will be up to you to figure out what works best for you. But for the

sake of this book, journaling will be an everyday practice for the next 7 days. Showing up everyday for the journaling exercises would be ideal, but it's okay to remember to hold grace for yourself. If you skip a day, a week or can't stay consistent, be mindful to hold grace for yourself and know that you are doing the best that you can in the moment. When you are ready, just come back to where you left off.

Before we get started with our daily journaling exercise, place your journal and pen in a location in a place that you will remember, and will have easy access to. You wouldn't want to skip a day or a moment of journaling because you misplaced your journal. Give your journal a home in your home so you will know where it is at all times. In this chapter I will share journaling exercises, but remember, you can journal any time you please, you don't have to wait for the prompts in this book.

Make your journaling an experience. This is a time to practice mindfulness. As you go through the journaling exercise, start to be mindful of how you enjoy journaling. Do you like to journal while sitting in bed ? Or maybe you prefer to journal while sitting outside in the elements of nature. Perhaps you enjoy sipping on a cup of " Becoming Unique" tea (shameless plug) while sitting at your kitchen table with your journal. Maybe sitting in your local cafe is the experience that floats

your boat. There is not one way to do things, but it's up to you to find out what resonates with you. Be open to trying different experiences. Try your best to be present with your journaling experience and not just do it for the sake of the book. Be Present and be mindful during this experience.

Are you ready ?

Each day over the next seven days, you will have a prompt to start writing in your journal. There is no wrong or right way to journal so remove the pressure of trying to do things right. Your journaling entry could be 1 sentence or 100 sentences and it could look different from day to day. Just write with your truth. There is no one to impress, this is personal experience with yourself.

The next page will have the seven days of journaling prompts on one page. You are not required to go in order. You can pick whatever prompt resonates with you that day. Be sure to go through all seven prompts. It's okay to repeat prompts, and it's okay to take more than seven days to complete this section.

Seven Days of Journaling Prompts

Day 1 of journaling prompt

Why do you feel adding self care into your life is important?

Day 2 journaling prompt

Thought Dump (Dump your thoughts today. How are you feeling, what's on your mind..... Just dump it)

Day 3 journaling prompt

List things that bring you joy or happiness and explain why?

Day 4 journaling prompt

Talk about your childhood, what parts do you remember most?

Day 5 journaling prompt

Write goals and ideas that you have for yourself (no goal or idea is impossible write)

> **Day 6 journaling prompt**
>
> *Gratitude entry*
> *(write all that you are grateful for and why)*

> **Day 7 journaling prompt**
>
> *Freestyle*
> *(the ball is in your court, write whatever you want)*

There are endless possibilities when it comes to journaling. The past seven days was to just get the ball rolling. If you enjoy having journaling prompts to get your juices flowing, the internet is a great resource to search for journaling prompts. Maybe you can make it a ritual to internet search 7 journal prompts on a weekly basis so you are prepared ahead of time on your journal entries. Maybe you prefer free flow or thought dumping whatever groves your fancy. Be mindful to do what resonates for you. Journaling is very personal and remember you can use journaling in a way to work though your problems by just writing them down. Try it.

We are closing out the journaling chapter now. Just a reminder, we will not talk about journaling in the following chapters, but be mindful to continue the practice just as you have been

continuing the practice of your affirmations. Be mindful of thinking about how you will add journaling to your lifestyle when you are not prompted. Can you add it into your morning routine or maybe your night routine ? Do you carry your journal with you on the go so you can journal when you are out at a cafe ? Be conscious of what resonates and feels good for you.

Let's now take a moment to applaud yourself for the work you have done in this chapter. You are Amazing. Maybe you could treat yourself to a treat for your work. It could be a scoop of ice cream or a new lip stick color. Celebrate your work, and accomplishments. Putting the work in is not always easy so celebrate for showing up for you.

CHAPTER 4

Small acts of Self Care!!!!!!

Welcome to week 4. This week is going to be such a treat for you and your spirit. The chapter is all about actions with intention with small acts of self care. A lot of times when we think of self care, we think of spa treatments with facials and manicures, and yes that is a beautiful form of selfcare, but those acts are not in this book. Small acts of self care will be about small actions that you can do on a regular basis without booking an appointment somewhere or spending money. These actions are about lifting our spirits with what we have.

On the following pages will be seven small acts of self care. You are not required to do them in order. Over the next seven days

be mindful to put intention in your small acts of selfcare. Feel free to do multiple acts of self care in the same day, there's no limit. You are the creator of your life experience and do what works for you. The one rule that I ask that you do for this section is to move with intention. At the end of the evening, be able to reflect back on your small acts of self care. When you move with intention it leaves memories. Be able to remember what you did and it will not be a forgetful experience.

Seven Days of
Small acts of Selfcare

> Day 1 (Small acts of self care)
> *Take a new route*
> *(Shake the energy up by traveling a new road today)*

In your travels today rather it be to work, the supermarket or school.... Take a different route out of your normal routine. When we move in the same way our energy could become stagnant, things are the same old same old experience that we could do it with our eyes closed. Walking or driving down a new road that we've never traveled before heightens our senses. You see houses or buildings that you have never seen before, and you never know what you may discover. Maybe there is a cafe that you never knew existed or a yoga studio that you may decide you want to take a class from. Perhaps your creative juices get flowing because you crossed a new environment that inspired you.

As you travel your new road, be mindful, take in your surroundings, how do you feel? Would you travel this road again? Be one with the experience, and be mindful of the chitter

chatter that may go on in the mind. If your mind is thinking about what someone said to you two weeks ago, it's stealing from the experience of being present with the experience of the new roads traveled.

Day 2 (Small acts of Selfcare)
Say something beautiful to yourself in the mirror

Look in the mirror first thing in the morning before you get glammed up. Look at yourself in your purest form with no distractions. Look at yourself eye to eye and say beautiful messages to yourself. Say' "I am beautiful in the very moment", "I am enough", "I love myself" This is a moment to be with yourself and acknowledge you.

Many times we look for the outside to validate us, to tell us we are beautiful or we are loved. This is your moment to validate yourself and not look for the outside to do it.

Brew your tea or coffee and sit. This is not a moment to have your tea/coffee on the go but a moment to be still and sit with your hot beverage. Be okay with just sitting with your drink. There is so much magic in stillness. Be still in the moment with no distractions, see what thoughts pop up in your head, be mindful to address thoughts as they come. If they are creative or new ideas, write them down. If negative thoughts arise, redirect the thought with mindfulness. Don't give negative thoughts power, negative thoughts are powerless when we give them no attention. Smile at happy thoughts.

A great way to get to know someone is to go out for a walk with them. You engage in a lot of random conversation which tells you a lot about the other person. You also get to see what sparks their interest by what they are commenting on during your travels and so on. Now it's time to enjoy time with you. Be

mindful of the conversations that you are having with yourself. What's sparking your interest during your walk?

Take a walk with yourself when you have a free moment and not under the pressure of a time contract. Be free in your walk without the pressure of you only have 10 minutes to be somewhere energy. Take your walk at a time where you are okay with not having a schedule

Day 5 (Small acts of Self care)
Move Your Body and Dance

Moving your body is a form of self care. If you already move your body on a regular basis through working out or dancing, you are such a rockstar, Keep moving your body. If you struggle to be consistent with moving your body, this is your opportunity to get up and move. It's sometimes hard to break out of old habits or to start new habits, but remember to always to give yourself grace no matter what part of your journey you happen to be on. Everyday is a new opportunity to start or to bring in change. Remember the one rule I have in this section is to act with intention. If you are already a mover and workout and dance often, maybe look into a new form of movement, try something new. If trying a new style of movement sounds

like too much work, dance or move to a different style of music than your usual style. Shake the energy up on your movement experience, we want to awaken deeper parts of you. If movement is not usually in your lifestyle , just DANCE. Dance like nobody's watching. If you feel comfortable in your body to dance in front of others, it's okay to bring others in. maybe dance with a friend, your partner, your kids.....with whomever that you dance with make sure you still feel yourself while dancing. Dancing with someone is not a requirement, it's just a suggestion if it floats your boat. Move with intention and make this a rememberable moment.

Day 6 (Small acts of Self care)
Eat or Cook something new

We are creatures of habit, and most times it rings true with the foods that we eat. We go to the supermarket and our grocery list is pretty much the same from week to week. When you go out to eat, how often do you try something new ? It"s okay to give yourself permission to try something that you have never had before. Hold no expectation and be open to try something new to eat. It doesn't have to be an extreme choice, it could be as simple as changing the ice cream flavor. If you always buy

chocolate ice cream, be open to experience a new flavor like strawberry. Make it an experience, and be intentional. If you do something like change your ice cream flavor, set a time to enjoy. Maybe buy special toppings for it. Be mindful of the flavor, does it remind you of anything? Do you like the flavor? Will you try this flavor again? These are examples of the type of questions you can ask yourself as you eat your new flavor of ice cream. Make memories with yourself. You DON'T have to have this perfect memory with no flaws. Make memories while experiencing life. Some things you will love, and some things may not be so great, but we have to experience different parts of life to understand what we love and what resonates with us and be okay when things are not perfect. Just focus on experiencing life. Try something New to Eat or Cook!

> ### Day 7 (Small acts of Self care)
> *You Decide what a small act of*
> *self care looks like for you personally*

It"s you turn to think about what resonates to you as a small act of self care in your life personally. Examples of other small acts of self care that you can try if you can't think of your personal one yet.

-If you are a person always on the go, giving yourself a moment of stillness is a form of self care.

-If you have been really restrictive with your eating habits, maybe treating yourself to that piece of cake could be an act of self love.

Be in tuned with what brings you joy without leaving you feeling guilty. It's always okay to make time and space for you. You can't pour from an empty cup so fill your cup first.

Before we head off to Week 5 Chapter 5, lets recap with some accountability questions

- » Have you included affirmations in your lifestyle?
- » How often do you journal?
- » Have you embodied the small acts of self care?
- » Would it interest you to rcap your small acts of self care in your journal entry?

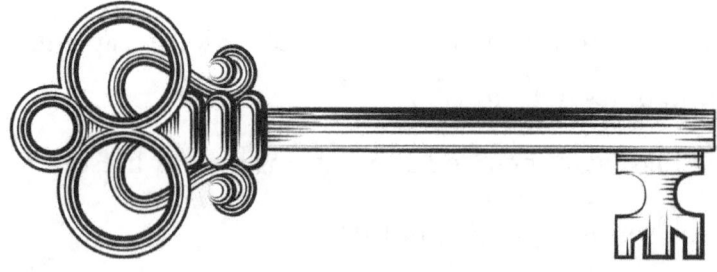

CHAPTER 5

Breathing!!!!!!

Let's start this Chapter with a DEEP BREATH.

Relax, feel comfortable in your body, when you are ready, take a deep inhale through your nose, full your lunges up, hold for a couple of seconds (if a couple of seconds is too long, be sure to release when you feel you have reached your max) then take a big exhale with your mouth open, its okay to make noise when you exhale through your mouth. Take this deep breath two more times which will be a total of three deep breaths.

How do you feel? Be mindful of how you feel after this breathing exercise.

Our breath is one of the most important elements of us in this human form. The first sign of life is when a baby takes its first breath, and the last sign of life is when a person takes its last breath. Without breath there is no life. Since our breath holds so much importance, let's be mindful to take intentional focus on our breath.

Many of us go to the gym or move our body in other ways to stay fit. Many of us watch what we eat so we can maintain our health. How many of us have thought about the health of our breath? Before reading this chapter, when was the last time you put intention on your breath? Rather you are a newbie at breathwork or a pro, this chapter (week) is about bringing focus and energy around your breath.

If you are reading this book, you are alive which means you are breathing right now. The breath you are using right now is an unconscious breath which means you are not thinking about it. This breath is a shallow breath. We are all masters at shallow breathing. The goal for this chapter is to work on a conscious breath, a breath with intention. When you started this chapter, you started with taking three deep breaths. You were very conscious when taking the deep breaths. You were in the moments of breathing, you felt your lungs expanding. When you start to add more deep breathing into your lifestyle

it allows more air to flow through your body and can calm your nerves, which in turn reduces stress and anxiety.

Just as moving your body and eating well are forms of self care. Taking care of our breath is a form of self care too.

If you have a smartphone, download some breathing apps. I will not promote or suggest any apps in this book, but I suggest you try a few out to see which one resonates with you. The goal for this week is to set 5 minutes aside each day to take a few deep breaths. Then sit in the stillness after doing your breathing exercises. If you download the apps, they do a great job with directing you through your breathing exercise. With the apps you will also have more breathing style options than the one deep breath that I offered at the beginning of this chapter. Also be sure to set the notifications on the breathing app if you want to get a daily reminder to breathe. If you don't have access to getting an app, just do the breathing exercise that I offered at the top of this chapter. As you start to work on your breath regularly, you will begin to be able to hold your breath for more than a couple of seconds, your stamina will get stronger.

Below you will simply just check off a list for 7 days to give yourself the accountability to show up to breathe on a deeper level.

BREATHWORK

- ☐ **Day 1. Breathe**

- ☐ **Day 2. Breathe**

- ☐ **Day 3. Breathe**

- ☐ **Day 4. Breathe again**

- ☐ **Day 5. Breathing is important! Breathe**

- ☐ **Day 6. Breathe again**

- ☐ **Day 7. Breath is life, be sure to take care of your breath**

This is the end of the BREATHING chapter, but not the end of your breath workout. You are the creator of your life. Be sure to create space to breathe on a daily basis.

There is a quote by Mike Murdock that says " The secret to your future is in your daily routine"

Learning to take a deep breath holds so many beneficial elements from decreasing stress to expanding our lungs. Consider working on your deep breathing daily to enjoy all of the fruits that deep breathing has to offer on a regular.

CHAPTER 6

Guided Meditation!!!!!

And we have arrived at the week of meditation. Did you know this was coming?

Meditation could be challenging for many people. It's a place of stillness, and in the world we live in with non stop stimulation happening, it could be hard to take it down and be still. My advice is to honor yourself with grace as you enter the realms of meditation. No pressure to look for perfection because that doesn't exist. If you already have a meditation practice, still walk through this chapter with your heart open to possibly expanding your practice.

There are many types of meditations, walking meditation, sound meditation, dancing meditation, guided meditation..... Your goal is to find out what style of meditation works for you. Be open to work on a meditation practice. Many times in life we have to try on more than one shoe until we find a comfortable fit.

Meditation could feel challenging because our minds love to do this thing called chitter chatter and it's up to us to be mindful of the chitter chatter, and address and redirect our mind. Guided Meditation is a great way to get started with meditation and if you already have a meditation practice, it doesn't hurt to add more options.

Adding a meditation practice to your lifestyle holds some beautiful benefits. Here is a list of some of the many benefits of meditation

> » Helps you to focus on the present
> » Reduces negative thoughts
> » Helps with creativity and imagination
> » Helps with patience
> » Helps with skills to manage stress and stressful situations

Can I tell you Something ? This very book that you are reading came from a meditation moment. I was in a guided meditation zoom call, and an idea for this book came. This is proof that beautiful things come from being still in meditation.

What is Guided Meditation? Guided Mediation is a type of meditation led by another person or an audio recording.

We are so lucky to be living in an era where we can have access to a guided meditation in the matter of a few moments via the internet. For the purpose of this book, I will ask that you take advantage of the internet to find guided meditations that resonate for you. On the following page you will see a list of how much guided meditation you should do for each day. You are welcome to do more, but try your best to do the minimum.

Before we Jump right into our guided meditation practice, please remember to hold grace for yourself. The list below is a guide, but not a requirement. If you skip a day, no sweat, just pick back up where you left off. Be open to play around with different guided meditations, you don't have to listen to the first one you find. Listen to different voices and tones to see which meditations you vibe with. This is your personal practice, the more you put in the more you receive back.

Remember at the beginning of the book when I said take inventory of your space. It's time to put that preparation to work. Be mindful to meditate where you have time and space with no distractions.

GUIDED MEDITATION 7 DAY LIST

Day 1
5 Minute Guided Meditation

Day 2
5 Minute Guided Meditation

Day 3
10 Minute Guided Meditation

Day 4
10 minute Guided Meditation

Day 5
15 Minute Guided Meditation

Day 6
15 Minute Guided Meditation

Day 7
20 Minute Guided Meditation

Congratulations on practicing Guided Meditation for one week. Please give yourself an applaud for showing up for you. If you missed a day or two of meditation, remember to give yourself grace, and applaud yourself for the days you did show up. Introducing new habits could be challenging when it comes to being consistent and it's okay. Do your best and don't look for perfection instead honor your progress.

Here are some questions to ask yourself following the completion of this chapter

1. How do you like guided meditation?
2. Will you continue to practice guided meditation?
3. Did you find a favorite guided meditation person to listen to?
4. What time frame do you prefer in listening to guided meditation?
5. Did you experience noteworthy experiences durings guided meditation?

Take notes on your guided meditation experience to understand what resonates with you. Asking yourself the above questions helps you understand your experience so you can understand how to customize your practice for your life. In the next chapter we will continue with mediation a little deeper.

CHAPTER 7

Meditation!!!!!

Last Chapter was a focus on guided meditation but this chapter will be a focus on meditation in general with an introduction to other forms of meditations such as walking meditation, sound meditation....

Meditation is such a beautiful tool to have in your lifestyle that I wanted to make sure we explore it deeper. In turn it will open the door of options on how to customize meditation to fit in your personal experience of life.

Over the next 7 days we will explore sound meditation, walking meditation and being still in your own silence meditation.

A quick reminder before we jump into our meditation flow days. Have you kept up with your affirmations, Journaling, small acts of self care and breathing discussed in the previous chapters? Remember to hold grace for yourself. It may sound overwhelming to keep up with, but remember don't seek perfection, seek progress. You don't have to show up for every task everyday, but start to be mindful of how you can start to incorporate newer tasks.

Let's Meditate

Day 1 Meditation
10 minute Walking meditation

Walking Meditation is all about letting yourself experience your surroundings and allowing yourself to notice things in that moment.

To start your walking meditation, first carve out a time in your schedule when you will be available to walk with no distractions. Your walking meditation will be a very present walk, it will be all about whis is happening in this very moment, not about what you should cook for dinner. You can start off walking by noticing your feet moving and say left foot, right foot as they move. Notice your environment. Are there trees, how are the

leaves shaped? Are the leaves swaying in the wind? Touch the grass, how does it feel against your skin, how does it smell? These are some examples of questions you can ask yourself to help you stay present in the moment. When you notice your mind drifting, bring it back to the moment that you are in. Be Present, Feel and Embrace your walking meditation.

Day 2 Meditation
10 minute Sound meditation

Sound Meditation is all about clearing the mind to help deepen your meditation. Music is multidimensional linking realms of the brain to help you with meditation.

Use your internet search to find a sound meditation to resonate with you. Play around with different sounds and notice your meditation. Make sure you carve out a time in your day to do your 10 minute sound meditation. Sit or lay down, find what's comfortable for you. Get in a position where you won't fall asleep. Laying down is fine if you know you wont fall asleep, but if you do fall asleep laying down, choosing a sitting position may be more suitable for you. When you are ready to meditate, turn your sound meditation music on, close your eyes and be. When chitter chatter starts to happen, hold grace and redirect

it. Be present and catch your mind when it starts to run in all types of directions.

> ### Day 3 Meditation
> #### *5 minute Meditation*

Meditation is all about being still, letting go of the chitter chatter in your mind and embracing mindfulness. Be mindful of your thoughts as they come and redirect them. Work on making the mind quiet. During your 5 minute meditation, remove all distractions, turn music & tv off. Put your phone far away, maybe in another room. You don't want to hear notifications popping up on your phone as you work on your meditation practice. Get in your comfortable position, close your eyes and be mindful. Hold Grace for yourself, and meditate.

> ### Day 4 Meditation
> #### *15 Minute Sound meditation*

> ### Day 5 Meditation
> #### *15 minute Sound Meditation*

> ### Day 6 Meditation
> #### *20 minute Walking meditation*

Time to give yourself a round of applause. You are really showing up for yourself. You didn't just complete this chapter but you have been putting focus and energy into your self care for 7 weeks now. No matter if you opened this book every day and did every single task, or if you held grace for yourself and showed up when you could, you are such a ROCKSTAR!!!!!! Keep up the great work and remember baby steps are still steps.

CHAPTER 8

Movement!!!!

Movement is important on so many levels. Many times movement is advertised for vanity reasons. Do this workout to get a six pack or a bigger butt. How many times have heard someone say, they have to go to the gym so they can work on their summer body.... This is all great and not knocking it, but lets embody movement in this book on a different level. Lets put intention on moving our body, just as we make time and space to eat everyday. It's time to be mindful of moving your body just a little bit more. If you are a mover and shaker in your body already. Use this chapter to explore new ways of moving your body. Exploring new ways of moving could be adding stretching into your life or taking extended intentional walks.

In this chapter I will guide you with simple suggestions on ways to incorporate more movement in your everyday lifestyle. You are not required to wear fancy workout clothes, go to the gym, or take a workout class. The only requirement is to move with intention and to hold grace for yourself. With holding grace for yourself in this chapter is to know your limits. The movements are suggestions and not requirements. If you feel a stretch or movement is more than what your body is willing to do, be sure to honor where you are at. A reminder that your self care is personal to you, which includes the way you decide to add movement.

Day 1 Movement
Stretch

Stretch your body before you get out of bed. Sit up in your bed, you can sit with your feet on the ground or sitting upright in your bed. You find out what works best in your body. Once you are in your upright position, take your arms, reach them over your head, if you can interlock your fingers and reverse your hands, if the interlock is too much, just lift your arms straight up. Now lift your arms up to the sky and feel the stretch, then lean the stretch to the right side of your body for 3 seconds,

next shift to the left side for another 3 seconds. You can repeat the stretch a few times. Never push yourself beyond your limits, honor where you are at.

How did that stretch make your body feel?

Day 2
Walk

There is a quote that says "Walking is man's best medicine" If you are able to walk, walk please. We have discussed walking throughout this book in multiple chapters with ways of adding selfcare. Walking was suggested in small acts of self care chapter as well in the meditation chapter. Walking could be three selfcare acts all in one. One walk a day can cover a walking meditation, an act of self care and now movements of the body.

Move your body and go for a walk today.

Day 3
Stretch

Today you can stretch in bed, at your desk, on the couch......
You can do today's stretch anywhere. Today, do some neck

rolls. Sit upright, close your eyes and starting on your right side move your neck in circles. Make three full circles in the right direction, then reverse and make three full circles going to the left. Another reminder to honor where you are at.

We live in a day and time where elevators and escalators are a modern day luxury that has become a lifestyle for many. Today if you are capable instead of jumping on the escalator or waiting for the elevator, take the stairs. If your lifestyle does not have escalators or elevators and stairs are not a close access, maybe make an adventure to find stairs in your environment. Otherwise if stairs are not an option, do a stretch or go for a walk today.

Today put some upbeat music on and move. You don't have to get up and dance but just let your body sway and move naturally as you listen to the music. Let the music move the

energy in your body. Take mental notes, is your body moving side to side, is your foot tapping or are you bobbing your head? Just let the music naturally guide your body's energy.

Day 6
Walk

Remember walking is man"s best medicine. Walk with intention, maybe set a goal on your walking. Do you want to walk a certain amount of steps or a length of time? Whatever you decide, just walk.

Day 7
Stretch & Walk

Wake up and do the two stretches discussed in this chapter. The neck rolls and over head stretch from day one. Later in the day, go for a walk. Or customize your personal movement for today.

Applaud yourself for being mindful to move your body. Keep growing your movement practice. Go on the internet and

look up stretching videos to find more ways to incorporate stretching into your lifestyle.

Can you keep up with being intentional to move your body?

CHAPTER 9

Review!!!!!

The past eight weeks have been beautiful with you showing up for yourself! You are amazing, keep up the great work.

If all of the tools that have been introduced in this book are new to your lifestyle, it could feel overwhelming to be consistent, but remember to hold grace and space for you. It is okay to let go of perfection and celebrate your progress. For example if you only said affirmations to yourself one time last week, that is called beautiful progress if you come from a place of never saying any affirmations at all. You should acknowledge that.

If you have been keeping up with this workbook every single day and haven't skipped a beat, be sure you are applauding yourself along the way for constantly showing up for you.

This book is all about introducing healthy tools into your lifestyle for you to thrive in your relationship with yourself. It's up to you to personalize these tools for you. This book is a guide but not the last word in your lifestyle.

Chapter 9 week 9 is all about reviewing what we have gone over so far before we hit the final stretch of the content in this workbook. Sometimes we are so eager to move forward that we forget to embody what we have already done. Or there could be so much information that we become overwhelmed and loose pieces of what we have learned. Reviewing holds so much importance on so many levels. You will need your journal for the review section. For each chapter week, there will be list of questions that you will respond to in your journal. Ponder on the questions and be honest with yourself in your response. Answering these questions allows you to dig deeper into these tools. Lets review -

Day 1: Affirmations (week 2)

1. How often do you practice affirmations?

_____

_____

_____

_____

_____

2. Do you like to say affirmations? (expand on your answer if it is no, why?)

_____

_____

_____

_____

_____

3. Have you customized your own personal affirmations? (If the answer is no, Do you want or plan on customizing your own affirmations?

_____

_____

_____

_____

_____

4. When do you practice affirmations? (morning routine, random, when sad ?)

_____

_____

_____

_____

_____

_____

5. Do you listen to affirmations?

_____

_____

_____

_____

_____

6. What are your affirmation goals? (when do you want to practice affirmations, how often.....)

_____

_____

_____

_____

_____

_____

Day 2: Journaling (week 3)

1. How often do you journal?

_____

_____

_____

_____

2. Do you like journaling (expand on why you like to journal. If the answer is no, why is journaling not resonating with you?)

_____

_____

_____

_____

3. What type of journaling do you do, Journal prompts, thought dumping.....?

_____

_____

_____

_____

4. What are your journaling goals? (how often do you want to journal, what do you want to journal about, how do you want to add it into your life routine.......?)

_____

_____

_____

_____

_____

_____

_____

_____

5. How does journaling make you feel emotionally?

_____

_____

_____

_____

_____

_____

_____

_____

Day 3: Small acts of self care (week 4)

1. When was the last time you added a small act of self care to your day?

_____

_____

_____

_____

_____

2. Did you have a favorite *small act of self care* that you liked from chapter week 4 ?

_____

_____

_____

_____

_____

3. Can you list all of the small acts of self care that you did for yourself over the past two weeks?

_____

_____

_____

_____

_____

4. Is there a small act of self care that you want to do for yourself but haven't done it yet? What's stopping you from doing it?

_____

_____

_____

_____

_____

_____

_____

_____

_____

5. Can you make a small acts of self care bucket list?

_____

_____

_____

_____

_____

_____

_____

_____

_____

Day 4: Breathing (week 5)

1. Did you do any breathing exercises today?

_____

_____

_____

_____

_____

_____

2. How often do you do breathing exercises?

_____

_____

_____

_____

_____

3. Did you download breathing apps, and if so what app is your go to app?

_____

_____

_____

_____

_____

4. How do you feel after doing breathing exercises?

_____

_____

_____

_____

_____

_____

5. Has breathing exercises become part of your daily routine?

_____

_____

_____

_____

_____

_____

6. Do you have any breathing exercise goals?

_____

_____

_____

_____

_____

_____

Day 5: Guided Meditation (week 6)

1. Do you like guided meditation?

_____

_____

_____

_____

_____

2. What do you like about guided meditation?

_____

_____

_____

_____

_____

3. How does guided meditation make you feel?

_____

_____

_____

_____

_____

4. When was the last time you listened to guided meditation?

_____

_____

_____

_____

_____

_____

_____

_____

5. When will be the next time you listen to guided meditation?

_____

_____

_____

_____

_____

_____

_____

_____

_____

_____

Day 6: Meditation (week 7)

1. How often do you meditate?

_____

_____

_____

_____

_____

_____

_____

_____

_____

2. Do you have a favorite style of meditation?

_____

_____

_____

_____

_____

_____

_____

_____

_____

3. When was the last time you did a walking meditation?

_____
_____
_____
_____
_____
_____
_____
_____
_____
_____
_____

4. How do you feel emotionally after you meditate?

_____
_____
_____
_____
_____
_____
_____
_____
_____
_____
_____

Day 7: Movement (week 8)

1. Did you move your body with intention today?

_____

_____

_____

_____

_____

2. What is your favorite way to move your body? It can be any form of movement outside of the few forms of movement then that was talked about in the book?

_____

_____

_____

_____

_____

3. Do you plan on moving your body everyday with intention?

_____

_____

_____

_____

_____

4. Do you have movement goals?

_____

_____

_____

_____

_____

_____

_____

_____

5. How does your body feel when you move it?

_____

_____

_____

_____

_____

_____

_____

_____

_____

Final questions in general

1. Do these new action tools feel natural or forced?

_____

_____

_____

_____

_____

_____

_____

2. What tools do you feel you need to work on and what is your plan of action?

_____

_____

_____

_____

_____

_____

A reminder before we move on to the next chapter is that you are doing an amazing job with showing up for you. Keep up the good work. Remember small steps are still steps, keep going.

CHAPTER 10

Pamper Time!!!!!!

This week is going to be such a treat. Many times when we hear about self care we think of the bubble baths and we have finally arrived at that part of the self care rituals.

The Goal for this book was to work on building a strong foundation with some self care roots that started from the inside first.

Think about a plant. You must first plant and nourish the seed to make sure the roots grow. When you start to see the flower blossom, you can now pamper that flower. Always work on the roots first.

This week will be set up differently than the previous weeks. There will not be a daily check off of what task to do everyday. Instead there will only be one task and that is to create a special bath for yourself.

Grab your journal and write down what your dream bubble bath looks like. Does it have rose petals, bubbles, the smell of lavender, a cup of tea, a glass of wine? Are you reading a book or is the bath in the dark lit by candles? Look on the internet for bath inspirations. Create your fantasy bath in your head, then write it down on paper. Once you have your bath fantasy on paper, its time to plan it out. Write a list of what you need to make your fantasy become a reality. Do you need a bath tray, bath salts, what type of soap do you want to use? Put intention behind your purchases, look at different brands, learn about brands. Maybe support small local businesses where things have been handmade with love instead of mass produced. Create an experience to remember.

Once everything on your bath checklist is done, decide what day you will create your pamper experience. Try your best to plan it on a distraction free day, but I know that can be very hard when you have kids. Just remember to give yourself grace and know you are doing your best.

It's the day of your pamper bath, remember to set the mood, what music are you listening to, what is the aroma in the air? Will you say affirmation before getting in the bath?

Sit and enjoy your bath. Water is very healing and highly vibrational. Think high vibrational positive thoughts and enjoy this moment.

After your bath, keep the same energy going with your environment, what music is playing, what aruma is in the air? What oils will you moisturize your body with?

If a bath is not an option for you, you can also create other pampering experiences from a foot bath to a home facial. Same rule applies with doing everything with intention.

Once you have created your custom pampering experience rather it be a bath, foot bath or a home facial, take a moment to reflect on your pampering experience in your journal. Once you have reflected on your experience, you will be ready to move on to the next chapter.

Continue to practice finding ways to add your affirmation, journaling, small acts of self care , breathing, meditation, movement and pampering yourself. Its not an easy task to create new habits, but keep working on what resonates with

you. Try things, try again and try new ways of approaching these new tools in your lifestyle.

You are about to enter chapter 11 so this means you have been showing up for the work, keep up the great work you are phenomenal.

Chapter 11 will require your journal. How is your journal looking after 10 weeks? Is it time to put intentional effort into buying a new journal? If its time to buy a new journal please do so before entering into chapter 11 week 11.

CHAPTER 11

Excitement!!!!

What Brings You Excitement? Be honest with yourself!

Stillness may bring you excitement. Maybe you are a homebody and you find joy in being home.

The next person may be excited by being in over stimulated situations with lots of people.

Two very different forms of excitement, but equally the same amount of excitement depending on who is receiving what.

Society may sell and tell us that the excitement is at the party, but that may not be your reality. Your excitement may be reading a book, playing with children, taking care of senior

citizens..... The list can go on and on with many different ways that you may feel excited outside of thinking you should be a party animal to have fun or bring joy to your spirit.

This week you will dive deep in your thoughts and think about what excites you. Remember what excites you doesn't have to be what others are telling us what excitement is.

You will have journal prompts every other day to help you dig into what brings you fire. Honesty with yourself is key. Try your best to shed away what you have been told to like or what you should do and how you should feel. This journey is only between you and you, you are free to be you. You have the permission to be you and not hold on to others expectations of what they think you should be and act like. BE YOU!!!!!!

On the day when you are not journaling, You will be prompted to go into meditation and be mindful of the thoughts that come up about you and your fire. Being still and quiet brings settled answers and insight, be mindful to pick up on the messages that you may receive during your meditations.

Day 1

Sit in meditation, be still (Be mindful to pay attention to messages that you may or may not receive during meditation. Don't look for messages, just be still and present)

Day 2

{Journal prompt} What does excitement mean, and look like to you? Dive deep, talk about excitement like you have never talked about it before

_____

_____

_____

_____

_____

_____

_____

_____

_____

_____

_____

_____

_____

_____

Day 3

Sit in Meditation, be still (again, don't look for answers or messages just be one with your meditation. If a message comes up, write it down)

Day 4

{Journal prompt} What activities brought you joy as a child? Dive deep, be honest, your answers don't have to look like what you think they need to look like.

_____

_____

_____

_____

_____

_____

_____

_____

Day 5

Sit still in meditation (Be still but listen)

Day 6

{ Journal prompt } Think about recent times when your heart felt full of joy, time flew and moments when you laughed. Write about these moments, and ask yourself, why did these moments bring me joy? Did these moments have things in common?

_____

_____

_____

_____

_____

_____

_____

Day 7

{ Journal prompt } What brings you joy ? What actions make you feel excited?

_____

_____

_____

_____

_____

_____

CHAPTER 12

Your Happy Place!!!!!!

Last chapter (chapter 11) I wanted you to put focus on what excites you. Hopefully you have arrived to understand what excites you. If you have come to an awareness of what excites you, you have arrived at the start of your *Happy Place*. If you are still trying to figure out what burns your fire, keep working on chapter 11 before continuing with chapter 12. It's perfectly okay to sit in chapter 11. When being honest with yourself, it's sometimes hard to find our truth at the core. Be okay with being STILL until what you are seeking comes.

If you are ready to continue in this week 12, chapter 12

CONGRATULATIONS, you have arrived at your HAPPY PLACE.

You have started to create a routine of Self Care and you understand what excites you. When you understand what burns your fire and brings you excitement, you start to have an understanding on what direction to move towards your happy place.

Arriving doesn't mean the journey is over, but instead you are on a new journey of working to fulfill your personal Happy Place. Work could be hard when we want life to just be easy, but remember there are some beautiful payoffs, and benefits that come along with consistent work.

This book has been about actions of pouring into yourself with tools like affirmations, journaling, small acts of self care, breathing, meditations, and so much more. Be mindful to keep pouring into yourself so your cup can overflow for others to receive all that you have to offer. It's not selfish to invest, and pour love into yourself first.

Let's end this book off with a few affirmations.

"I deserve to love myself first"

"I deserve to be happy"

"I deserve to enjoy the fruits of my labor"

Keep up the amazing work! This book is just a kick start, but the work is in your daily routine. You can always come back to this book at any time for a restart or a refresher.

"You hold the key to your life's journey"

Journaling Pages

for You

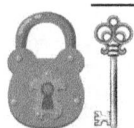

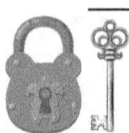

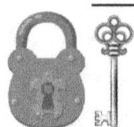

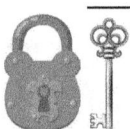

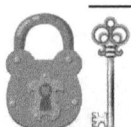

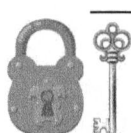